Kate's Grandma

Rusty's Cookies

Barbara Hoskins

OXFORD
UNIVERSITY PRESS

Oxford University Press
198 Madison Avenue, New York, NY 10016, USA
Great Clarendon Street, Oxford OX2 6DP, England

Oxford New York
Athens Auckland Bangkok Bogotá Buenos Aires Calcutta Cape Town
Chennai Dar es Salaam Delhi Florence Hong Kong Istanbul Karachi
Kuala Lumpur Madrid Melbourne Mexico City Mumbai Nairobi Paris
São Paulo Shanghai Singapore Taipei Tokyo Toronto Warsaw

and associated companies in
Berlin Ibadan

OXFORD is a trademark of Oxford University Press.

ISBN 0-19-436446-1

Editorial Manager: Shelagh Speers
Senior Editor: Sherri Arbogast
Editor: Lynne Robertson
Assistant Editor: Christine Hartzler
Production Editor: Mark Steven Long
Elementary Design Manager: Doris Chen Pinzon
Designer: Ruby Harn
Senior Art Buyer: Patricia Marx
Art Buyer: Elizabeth Blomster
Production Manager: Abram Hall

Printing (last digit): 10 9 8 7 6 5 4 3

Printed in Hong Kong.

Original character art by Dora Leder
Illustrations by Bill Colrus and Lane Gregory
Other illustrations by Jim Talbot

Cover design by Doris Chen Pinzon/Natacha Menar
Cover illustration by Bill Colrus and Lane Gregory

For Taka and Miku.

Kate's Grandma

"This is my grandma's house," says Kate.
"Wow!" says Jenny.

grandma = grandmother

"This is my grandma's dog," says Kate.
"It's purple!" says Jenny.

dog

Jenny and Kate go to the kitchen.
"Cookies!" says Kate.
"They're purple!" says Jenny.

"Here," says Kate.
"No, thank you," says Jenny.

kitchen

cookies

Jenny and Kate go upstairs.
"Purple shoes!" says Jenny.

upstairs

shoes

"Look at these," says Kate.
"Wow!" says Jenny.

"Who's she?" asks Jenny.
"She's my grandma!" says Kate.

Jenny and Kate go outside.
"Hi, Grandma."
"Hello, Kate."

outside

"This is my friend, Jenny," says Kate.
"Hello, Jenny," says Grandma.
"It's nice to meet you."
"Hello," says Jenny. "It's nice to meet you, too."

"I like your house," says Jenny.
"Thank you," says Grandma.

"Your hair!" says Jenny.
"What?" asks Grandma.

hair

"It isn't purple," says Jenny.

"Purple hair?" says Grandma. "That's silly."

silly

13

Exercises

A. Match.

1. Grandma _C_

2. Kate ____

3. Grandma's dog ____

4. Jenny ____

a.

b.

c.

d.

B. Yes or no?

1. Kate's house is purple. ☐ Yes ☑ No

2. The cookies are brown. ☐ Yes ☐ No

3. Jenny and Kate go upstairs. ☐ Yes ☐ No

4. Grandma's hair is purple. ☐ Yes ☐ No

C. Fill in the blank.

1. Jenny is Kate's ___friend___.
   a. friend
   b. sister
   c. grandmother

2. Grandma's _____ is purple.
   a. hair
   b. dog
   c. desk

3. Grandma's _____ is not purple.
   a. house
   b. hair
   c. dog

4. Grandma is _____.
   a. purple
   b. upstairs
   c. outside

Rusty's Cookies

"John's here," says Sarah's mother.
"Hi, John."
"Hi, Sarah."

"Wow! You can bake cookies!" says John.
"Don't eat it!" says Sarah. "It isn't a cookie."

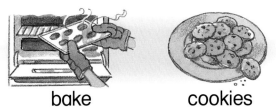

bake   cookies

"What is it?" asks John.
"It's a dog biscuit," says Sarah.
"It's for Rusty."
"Oh! They're Rusty's cookies!" says John.

dog biscuit

"Do you want a cookie?" asks Sarah.
"Yes, I do," says John.

"Here you are," says Sarah.
"Thanks!"

thanks = thank you

"Where's Rusty?" asks John.
"I don't know," says Sarah.

"Look! There he is!" says John.
"He's in the backyard."
"Let's go!" says Sarah.

backyard

"Hi, Mrs. Smith," says Scott.

"Hi, Scott," says Mrs. Smith.

"Is Sarah here?" asks Scott.

"Yes, she is," says Mrs. Smith.

"Sarah and John are in the kitchen."

kitchen

"Cookies! I like cookies!" says Scott.

"Yuck!" says Scott. "What is this?"

yuck

"It's not a cookie!" says Sarah.
"It's a dog biscuit!" says John.

"I'm sorry, Rusty," says Scott.
"This is for you."
"Woof!"

sorry   woof

Exercises

A. Match.

1. cookie __b__

2. dog biscuit ____

3. backyard ____

4. kitchen ____

a.

b.

c.

d.

B. Yes or no?

1. Sarah can bake dog biscuits. ☐ Yes ☐ No

2. Rusty's cookies are dog biscuits. ☐ Yes ☐ No

3. Scott is in the backyard. ☐ Yes ☐ No

4. The dog biscuits are for Scott. ☐ Yes ☐ No

C. Fill in the blank.

1. Sarah can bake __dog biscuits__ .
   a. ice cream
   b. dog biscuits
   c. rice

2. The dog biscuits are for _____.
   a. John
   b. Sarah
   c. Rusty

3. Rusty is _____.
   a. a dog biscuit
   b. a dog
   c. a backyard

4. Mrs. Smith is Sarah's _____.
   a. mother
   b. sister
   c. friend